Tranquil Hearts

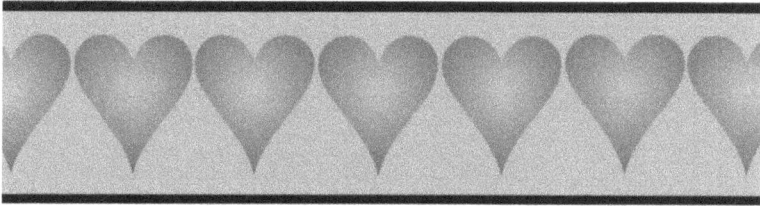

Romantic Poems
Of Love by
Dexter L. Monroe

Tranquil Hearts

ISBN: 978-0-6151-7244-6

Tranquil Hearts

Table of Contents

Continued

Tranquil Hearts

Eternal Chains

O' that gentle passionate kiss
Stirring our hearts in bliss
Great is our love without fail
Like to two ships together we'll sail

Beyond the curtain of night
We'll twine together in flight
Never to doubt or run
Blended with thoughts we've spun

Clothed with loves true cape
Sheltered by loves true fate
Upon this we dine and sip
Yearning to capture each drip

This burning temptation forever
Shall guide us through every endeavor
Our thought's we'll share the same
Loving in blissful gain

Our love forever shall endure
A love so deep and pure
With loving smiles and grins
Our love shall never end

Dexter L. Monroe

River Of Love

Like a gentle flowing river
Our love shall always flow
With the spoken words I love you
Just to let you know

Each day we'll find our happiness
In everything we share
Sharing our thoughts together
Giving in loving care

Life has wondrous treasures
This we found so true
Side by side together
Only loving you

Living each day and knowing
This wondrous gift of bliss
Holding each other for hours
Never a day we'll miss

Streams of wonder and beauty
Will bless our love so great
I am ever so happy and thankful
To be your loving mate

Dexter L. Monroe

Throne Of Love

Such a beauty I've never known
For our love is like a thrown
Its lasting power we'll share
Built with the love we bare

Solid and stately secure
Through time it will always endure
Held by loves true gold
For us to have and hold

For this world we'll keep at bay
With our love day by day
Sharing that throne forever
Nothing could ever be better

Perfected by love and deed
Crowned by loves true seed
Lasting eternal and strong
Our love will keep us from wrong

Dedicated to be as one
Our throne of love is done
For now and forever to keep
This love we share so deep

Dexter L. Monroe

The Very First Day

From the very first day we meant
I felt you were heaven sent
With each word we shared I knew
My heart would belong to you

For time had opened the door
For a love to bloom once more
Hearts so perfectly a lined
Forever our love will bind

So passionate is this love we share
Nothing will ever compare
A love so deep and devout
Our hearts doth sing and shout

Forever our love will say
It was meant to be each day
Sharing this love we know
Forever will it grow and grow

For with out a doubt we know
Our love forever will show
For each day we'll work to keep
A love so dear and sweet

For time will pass on by
But our love shall never die
The flames of love we feel
Forever we'll keep so real

Dexter L. Monroe

Life's True Treasure

O' how I cherish your love each day
For it's in every smile you cast my way
Those eyes of contentment that linger long
It's a message of love so deep and strong

The slightest touch or long embrace
So captive with love my heart doth race
That lingering kiss with affection and zeal
Illuminates my soul with a love so real

This wonderful gift you share with me
A love eternal forever to be
Even in times when we're far apart
Your love is still close within my heart

To know such a love so rare and true
Forever my heart will belong to you
For every moment you fill my thoughts
How thankful I am for the love we've wrought

For it's pure of heart and ever true
Bathed with each kiss like morning dew
Your beauty sets my heart a glow
I love you so deeply, I want you to know

For life gives treasures now and then
You're my treasure where life begins
Your luminous love that lights my way
Forever shall it dwell in my heart to stay

Dexter L. Monroe

Symphony Of Love

In symphony our hearts doth play
Songs of love each day
With melody's of loves great roar
Our hearts forever will soar

So high our love doth fly
Beyond the sun drenched sky
With loving song's of bliss
We share in loves true gift

Forever these songs we'll hear
Drawing our hearts so near
With loving hearts we'll dance
To songs of true romance

With thunder we'll feel each beat
With a love so dear and sweet
Then softly our minds will hear
Songs of our love so pure

For each day we'll long to play
The symphony of love's display
With every caress and kiss
Forever will be our wish

The songs of love we'll hear
With every passing year
Sharing this love so strong
In the symphony of loving songs

Dexter L. Monroe

Flickering Candles

When ever a candle burns
Our hearts of love doth yearn
With every flickering flame
Our love is just the same

This fiery love we feel
Burns so deep and real
For deep within our hearts
Those flames of love impart

For candle wax doth burn
But our hearts forever will yearn
Sharing a love divine
Our love forever will shine

Some candles burn with scent
The aroma is finally spent
But the aroma of love we share
Forever will fill the air

So intense with loves true heat
Our passionate times will peak
The light of love we share
So magically burns with care

For every candle we light
Our love doth burn so bright
For one in heart and desire
We'll share in loves true fire

Dexter L. Monroe

Cherished Moments

O' how our hearts doth dance
With love and true romance
Our hearts are overwhelmed
With such a love we found

So pure and undefiled
Our hearts doth truly smile
For each day we yearn so deep
Forever this love we'll keep

This magic of loves true fire
We share with burning desire
Being one in heart and mind
Together forever in time

For every minute we'll know
This true love we both doth hold
With laughter and loves true play
We'll cherish those times each day

For in quiet times we'll kiss
Caressing in perfect bliss
Our passions will lead the way
As we power in loving play

Forever shall be our theme
Sharing our love and dreams
This wonderful love we know
Forever our hearts will hold

Dexter L. Monroe

Grains Of Sand

Nothing do I treasure more
Than you who I love and adore
For every wish came true
Finding some one like you

Through endless days and time
Our love began to rhyme
For our hearts now beat as one
Filled with loves true fun

The love in every caress
Sets our hearts to rest
To rest in loves true plan
Like endless grains of sand

Nothing shall sway our passion
To share in loves true fashion
To give our un-dying all
For this was fates true call

Our thoughts and every breath
Are shared and truly blessed
How perfect and pure is the taste
Of loves gentle grace

For time shall never slow
Our love will forever grow
Deeper we'll bond each day
Eternally through time to stay

One in heart and mind
Forever through the winds of time
Hand in hand we'll glide
Sailing on loves true tide

Dexter L. Monroe

A Life With You

I found a life so wonderful
Sharing each day with you
Knowing your loves forever
A love so pure and true

To see your loving smile
And feel your gentle touch
A heart felt hug that lingers
I love you O' so much

In every kiss we share
It thrills our very souls
A love so deeply shared
Never growing old

Hand in hand we'll walk
Sharing in every way
This love we share keeps blooming
Day after day

I will never find another
A love so sweet and true
Nothing could ever be better
Then spending my life with you

Dexter L. Monroe

Loves Blooming Flowers

Each flower that blooms in spring
Forever our hearts will sing
With rainbow colors and dew
Our love is forever renewed

The seeds of love we share
Are planted so deep with care
For our hearts are like the stems
With a love so strong within

With hearts we share the rain
That sparks our love to flame
Nurtured with every kiss
Our hearts are shared in bliss

For each day the sun doth shine
We'll toast to our love with wine
When clouds roll in with thunder
Our passion will heighten in wonder

For the clouds will roll away
And the night shall cover the day
For then our time will come
To frolic in loves true fun

With candles that dance and glow
We'll shed our leaves and grow
For the sun shall light the moon
Forever our love will bloom

Dexter L. Monroe

Cupids Darts

For this is ever so true
My heart belongs to you
Your countenance I truly adore
For you are my true Amore

Every smile you cast my way
My heart doth reel and sway
Filled with a love you impart
Delivered by Cupid's darts

O' such a love beyond control
Forever our love will blossom and grow
Hearts the same that bore our thoughts
Tied together with loves true knot's

The fire within that's truly shared
Forever we'll keep this love so rare
For each day we'll impart our words of love
Carried on the wings of loves true dove

Our passions will rage with every kiss
We'll power with love in total bliss
That yearning we both doth feel inside
Will rage forever as our love doth guide

O' my great lover forever to hold
Continually growing ever so bold
O' such a love and magic we share
We'll keep it forever in loving care

Dexter L. Monroe

The Gift Of Willows

Willows so strong yet bending
Bring forth a beauty un-ending
For our love is like the willow
Strong and yet so mellow

Girded with a sprawling base
So deep its routs give place
Those roots of love we embrace
Set our hearts to race

For the winds doth strengthen the limbs
And the leaves do flutter and hinge
On the winds of love we'll glide
Deep is this love we'll hide

With loving limbs we'll unfold
Sharing leaves of love un-told
For it covers our paths each day
Like Willows our loves displayed

Dexter L. Monroe

Dreams Of Reality

Once in a life time of dreams
One stands out serine
For one special dream finally came
Burning with a love un-tamed

For now it's blooming each day
With a fragrance, our hearts lock away
Never shall it cease to end
It grows deeper each day within

So sweet is this love we smell
Forever in our hearts it dwells
That yearning desire to share
This love we found so rare

For time hath found away
To guides us together to stay
This permanent bond we share
Fills our hearts with love and care

That care that brightly flickers
With words and poems we say
Like a candles towering flame
Our love doth burn the same

For our hearts are consumed each day
In every thoughtful way
For our love shall ever be
Cherished by you and me

Dexter L. Monroe

Dreaming Of You

Forever in my dreams I'll see
Pure love you brought to me
For hand in hand we'll glide
Through dreams of love we'll fly

So vivid and truly real
Our hearts are one and sealed
For nothing can stop our dreams
With a love that's so extreme

This power of love we share
Our dreams doth take us there
This magic of love we hold
We dream with love so bold

We frolic through forest's and fields
For each dream is truly so real
The beauty of colors we see
Forever your there with me

With laughter and smiles we play
Your there with me each day
With arms of love we caress
Sharing time to kiss and rest

Then passionate times arise
We share our love with pride
So perfect in everyway
In my dreams you'll always stay

Dexter L. Monroe

The Fountain Of Love

For the time has truly come
To share our bodies as one
Our love will be complete
Forever as our heart's doth beat

For they beat with passion and desire
With a love that burns like fire
Intensely romantic in thought
For this love we share so hot

For each moment we share in time
Our love will build and climb
Higher than the highest mountain
We'll share at loves true fountain

Flowing like a river wild
Forever our hearts will smile
That smile will guide our way
Through the heavens of our own play

This magical love we adore
Will keep us forever more
One in heart and soul
Eternally our love will grow

Far beyond loves true time
Our hearts as one shall rhyme
For this love we hold so dear
Forever will draw us nearer

Dexter L. Monroe

Heavenly Rays of Love

O' how preponderating is this love we share
How tenderly we caress it with gentle care
We grasp and hold minutes untold
To love and grow each day so bold
Our love forever unfolds

Nostalgic in nature is this love we entreat
Together as one forever so sweet
With amazing passion our love doth soar
Bestowed in our hearts with a lions roar

Untamed we give from dawn till night
We rest and sleep in cuddling delight
Our love is pampered each glorious day
In deed and hand and what we say

The words of love we utter so sweet
Sharing our hearts our love doth speak
Surprising with gifts and roses we say
Ever so thankful our loves displayed

Days will pass with years of embrace
Sharing so sweetly this love we doth taste
For our love will shine with heavenly rays
Showering our hearts, come what may

O' this great love that's born within
Bonded in heart our world doth spin
For ever our hearts will sing in praise
This beautiful love we share each day

Dexter L. Monroe

Love's True Rest

O' how magical this love we know
Shared so deep with loves sweet flow
Our passionate words shared so true
Coverth our hearts like morning dew

This love we hold and share in time
For this river of love doth truly bind
Hearts that beat each day in song
The song of love all day long

The power of this love so imparts
Forever so sealed within our hearts
Our thoughts so perfect in every way
For one in heart we think each day

Our hearts doth thunder with every kiss
For this love's beyond the mind could wish
Enchanting with peace and felt within
This magic of love will never end

Bonded so deep with love's true fire
Our hearts doth beat with one desire
Forever to be with time that flows
This love forever we shall always know

With night that falls on everyday
We'll show our love with love's sweet play
Then we'll share in loving caress
Together forever in loving rest

Dexter L. Monroe

Gentle Sounds of Love

The gentle sounds of love
Whispered in every breath we breathe
Consuming our total thoughts
Fulfilling our deepest needs

The tender words of love
Placed within our hearts
This magic we doth share
Never will depart

A love so strong and growing
Each and every day
Longing to be together
Sharing what we may

Dreams of holding each other
Loom with every hour
Patiently waiting to unfold
Like a spring booming flower

Hearts now locked and bonded
By everything we do
Longing for that gentle touch
Yearning to be with you

Our hearts are set to swoon
Dwelling on every kiss
Our love is so perfected
It rhymes in total bliss

Dexter L. Monroe

"I Do"

Our lives are truly touched
Each and every day
We hold to every kiss
In a very loving way

We yearn to be together
Never to be apart
Sharing our hopes and dreams
Its shared within our hearts

Our minds so perfectly a lined
A love so pure and true
The day that we we're married
Sharing the words " I Do"

Nothing will ever change this love
Nothing can brake its hold
We'll journey our lives together
Even when growing old

For this is my eternal prayer
That God will guide our way
Forever you'll always know
My heart's with you each day

Dexter L. Monroe

Loves True Mortar

Embracing each day that dawns
Great is this love we spawned
Like mortar and bricks it builds
For we share in loves true will

With magic our hearts doth give
Forever in love we'll live
For each hour we'll dream for more
Cleaving to this love we adore

For one in heart we'll stay
Side by side we'll play
In loves sweet games we'll share
Our loves beyond compare

For time has granted our way
This love to enjoy each day
With each smile we'll truly know
This love forever we'll hold

Our eyes doth twinkle each morn
With loves true magic performed
For our hearts can truly say
We're deeper in love each day

This beauty of love we share
Come from words of care
For time will spin on by
With hearts in love we'll fly

Dexter L. Monroe

Flight Of The Dove

One of life's greatest treasures
Is sharing my love with you
Striving to be together
In everything we do

I cling to every word
You share with me in love
True of thought and heart
Like the flight of a morning dove

Words I'll never find
To describe the way I feel
I love you O' so deeply
Forever a love so real

My eyes behold your beauty
Each and everyday
I yearn to hold thy countenance
In a very tender way

Forever shall I love you
Tranquility shared in bliss
A love so deeply nurtured
With every loving kiss

Dexter L. Monroe

Love From Above

Amazing is this love we found
A love that truly abounds
Like birds that chirp and sing
With love they let it ring

For our hearts begin each day
With words of love we say
Every wish and dream we share
Our hearts are one in prayer

The beauty and wonder of love
Comes from heaven above
So tenderly and deeply applied
In our hearts it doth abide

For time has made it so
This love we've come to know
For now it fills our hearts
Never shall it ever depart

The days and years shall pass
But our love forever will last
Growing ever so deeper in love
Sent to us from heaven above

For nothing will change my mind
In love I shall deeply reside
So this I can promise to you
Forever I'll always be true

Dexter L. Monroe

Picture Perfect Love

My adorable loving sweetheart
Our love will never part
Your beauty is beyond compare
My heart is yours to bare

Every moment my hearts with you
For your love will only do
For our love doth serge with power
In our minds this love devourers

So sweet and nutured with care
We share this love so rare
For our hearts are truly one
Nothing will rob our fun

For this love we hold up high
For others to see and sigh
Our love we'll truly display
For the world to see each day

Beyond my love for thee
Best friends we'll always be
True lovers in every way
For one in heart we'll stay

Bonded in loves true plan
Forever hand in hand
Sharing each day entwined
Our love forever will shine

Dexter L. Monroe

Molded As One

Never a day goes by
When I don't stop and sigh
Thinking of who I love most
It's of you I proudly boast

For love is more than feelings
It sets our hearts a reeling
For this captive love we share
Our hearts doth beat with care

For our hearts and minds become
Forever molded as one
Through time and space we found
Our love so truly abounds

For the minutes that pass on by
Our hearts doth speak and sigh
O' this great love we found
Forever our hearts doth pound

Forever each day we'll know
We're bonded with loves sweet flow
This love we know so deep
It's ours forever to keep

Dexter L. Monroe

Loves True Tide

Loves horizon is upon my eyes
That wondrous love that fills the sky
Forever illuminating my wanting heart
Knowing your love is heavens start

Eternal and blessed with loves pure hope
My heart doth ring with every note
Your adorning words grant my peace
With all your love completely released

You tame my longing of inner desires
For you hath granted me loves true fire
To walk with you in cherished steps
I shall never again have any regrets

Your love has kindled fires un-known
Just for me and me alone
I thirst each day for your loving caress
Sharing your kisses my hearts at rest

Captivating beyond the oceans tide
I'll journey with you on loves true ride
That eternal flow of loves true passion
Never wanting more than true old fashion

For our love shall never get replaced
We'll hold that love and run the good race
With hand and heart and every word
We'll drink from our love and never thirst

Dexter L. Monroe

Ribbons Of Love

Beyond the mind can feel
Even a touch that's real
Our hearts are interlaced
With ribbons of love we placed

To know a love so great
Know one could ever debate
For within our very souls
Forever we'll always know

For this love is truly a gift
Never to be a drift
Know one could ever imagine
This love they call old fashion

For ever to be as one
Sharing our love with fun
Nothing this world could say
Would cause my mind to sway.

This yearning my heart doth feel
Goes beyond even what's real
It burns so deep inside
It's a love I could never hide

For this love I share with pride
Forever at your side
Forever this love shall be
For my heart belongs to thee

Set your heart at peace
For our love shall never cease
With love I can truly say
I love you more each day

Dexter L. Monroe

Forever In Time

Profound and O' so true
Is this love I have for you
With the tides of mind I hold
This love so deep and bold

This wonder of love so real
My heart will ever feel
Through tulips we'll skip and play
With romance in every way

With hands we'll grasp so tight
Sharing in loves delight
For this excitement we feel within
This love shall never end

For our hearts doth truly swim
With this love so deep within
With hours I'll grant your way
I'll lift your heart each day

Beyond the stars of night
Our passion will burn so bright
For each moment we share and kiss
Our bodies shall rock in bliss

For each hour that fleets away
Our love will grow each day
Stronger our hearts will be
From this love I give to thee

Dexter L. Monroe

Loves Magic Knock

With every step through life
It can come with a little strife
With courage we forage on
True love can make us strong

For love some times we wait
Our minds doth ponder in debate
Through magic and the hand of fate
Love knocks to end the wait

For a love we found so true
With time it did ensue
Our hearts awakened one day
True love had come our way

So beautiful are the feeling inside
When our hearts were truly applied
For this love did truly bloom
The wait was over in gloom

The peacefulness of loves true gift
For never again we'll drift
For in love we truly know
Forever this love will grow

The passion we feel inside
With hearts as one we glide
This love forever did spawn
In love we share this bond

Dexter L. Monroe

Loving Thoughts

My deepest loving thoughts
Are those of being with you
To live each day forever
Nothing could be more true

Love has gently touched our hearts
So beautiful in every way
We yearn to hold and touch
Never to fade way

My dreams are filled each hour
Thinking of your loving smile
It glows with everlasting love
I ponder all the while

The romantic times we share
Inhaling a love so blessed
We cling to every minute
Never wanting to stop and rest

The softness of your kiss
your gentle caressing touch
I grasp to hold thy beauty
I love you O' so much

Our love so deep and strong
Bonded so deep true
This is my hope forever
Only to be with you

Dexter L. Monroe

Sweet Oil Of Amour

Within our hearts we hold
A love so gentle and bold
With honor and trust each day
Our love will deeply stay

With cruet in hand I'll pour
Sweet oil of gentle Amour
For this magic of love we share
Will carry us beyond despair

With every smile that's shed
Forever our hearts are feed
The love we both entreat
Forever we'll find so sweet

With a love that so serene
We'll share each others dreams
Our hearts will join in flight
Above the stars at night

For one in heart we'll brocade
A love that never fades
Intense and so divine
For upon this love we'll dine

Never shall our hearts dissuade
The path of life we made
With passionate hearts we'll soar
Sharing in true Amour

Dexter L. Monroe

Soaring Desires

Our hearts doth truly loom
With a fragrance of flowers in bloom
This love that reigns so bold
Deep in our hearts we hold

We hath willed our love complete
Forever it's ours to keep
To share and walk as one
Never to be un-done

Together we'll share our dreams
With hearts that truly beam
For our love is not a test
It's beyond the best and blessed

For each day our passion holds true
With hearts of love renewed
With un-tamed desires we'll share
Our love beyond compare

For limits shall not be placed
As we soar in loves true taste
For one in mind we'll rhyme
Our bodies will blend and twine

O' such a love we share
The fire our hearts doth bare
For truly our love's the best
In this we would confess

Dexter L. Monroe

Virtuous Love

O' what a virtue I've come to know
To be honored with a love that forever flows
Sweet to the smell like flowers in bloom
This love we share so passionately consumes

To sleep and share our bodies doth cling
Beholding loves magic our hearts doth sing
Romantically we drift among the stars
To forage deep, beyond even Mar's

Eternally we eclipse, eons of time
A love so cherished forever to rhyme
Our love transpires in music and song
A love so divine and kept so strong

For each bell that rings the angels doth sing
O' such happiness our love doth bring
For destiny bloomed with loves true fate
We'll share this love beyond heavens gate

For with every hug and melting kiss
Our love repeats to bore our wish
For thou hast made my life complete
Never shall I find a love so sweet

Dexter L. Monroe

Perfect Love

Each day we wake and know
The happiness we both share
A love that grows forever
Nothing shall ever compare

The gentle cry of love
Is pressed against our hearts
We share each day together
never to depart

We feel each day as one
Bonded with a loving kiss
We hold each other tenderly
Never a day we'll miss

Life for me is perfect
To live each day with you
Knowing our love is shared
A love so pure and true

Every gentle smile of love
Is shared with every hug
I shall never find another
O' such a love we discovered

Dexter L. Monroe

Cradled In The Arms Of Love

O' thou hast brought me such joy
With such fervor the love you employ
So immense my heart feels cradled
By your arms at loves true table

No dimness of loves true light
Follows my days nor night
Your love inspires my steps
For in my heart it's always kept

This shroud of love you endow
Like a painting calling aloud
So captive we soar within
Together in love we swim

This magic we share so real
Forever shall we always feel
For our love flows like a river
So intense our bodies doth quiver

Each touch kindles the fire
With flames of our loving desire
For now and ever to be
My heart hath I given to thee

Dexter L. Monroe

Hearts Of Loving Pride

I hear thee my love, calling my name
For our hearts are one and beat the same
That yearning desire we both doth feel
Pulls at our hearts like a magnet to steel

O' this wondrous love we bare
So deep, so sensual our hearts doth share
This captive love that came our way
It's truly refreshing like water each day

In moments of silence our passion doth roar
Our thoughts and hearts yearn for more
Ever so giving in this love we confide
For each moment together our hearts doth fly

This loves true world we share inside
Forever in this love we'll truly hide
Carried each day in every way
Ours hearts and minds will surely convey

Loves burning rage we feel so strong
Forever together we both belong
Bonded as one in true Amour
Together we'll soar through loves true doors

So enchanting we share this love with pride
With feelings so deep we could touch the sky
This stairway of love we found so sweet
In love forever our hearts doth beat

Dexter L. Monroe

Doors Of Love

When I think of all the ways
We share our love each day
So magical we both believe
Our love forever will be

For such a love as this
We know it's loves true gift
For the doors of love did open
It set our hearts in motion

So now this love we'll hold
For the doors of love won't close
This heavenly love we know
Through the doors of love it flows

Forever pouring through
This loves so pure and true
Eternally our hearts will sing
For upon this love we'll cling

This powerful love we share
We'll hold forever with care
For with loves true passion we'll fly
Day by day so high

So enchanting in every way
We embrace in love each day
This beauty of love so deep
Forever it's our's to keep

Dexter L. Monroe

Shores Of Eternal Bliss

From the shores of eternal bliss
We embrace each lingering kiss
Each kiss that holds its flavor
We yield our hearts and savor

Mingling our tongues with passion
Our lips entwine in fashion
Consuming with every breath
Bonded with loves true rest

Soaring with hearts in flight
Cresting in utter delight
Loving each other in madness
Filling our hearts with gladness

This waterfall of consuming lust
Gives us an eternal rush
Flowing with a mighty roar
We open loves true door

This blissful walk through time
We'll share as one sublime
Forever hand in hand
Our love will flow like sand

Dexter L. Monroe

Rush Of Love

O' this rush of love within
How it drives my every whim
For every waking hour
This love has so much power

Consuming my heart each day
Locked within to stay
How serene this feeling is
I long for every kiss

This passion we both now share
It lifts our hearts with care
Beyond loves golden sea
Forever our hearts will be

This towering love so sweet
Our hearts in unison beat
For time did stop that day
When true love came our way

Nothing shall ever divide
This love so deep inside
Forever this love will stand
With fates true loving plan

For our hearts doth truly swim
With a love so deep within
Forever our hearts will sing
With a rush of love we'll cling

O' this Rush of Love!

Dexter L. Monroe

True Love Born

O' that great day our love was born
Never again shall our hearts be torn
For one in heart we'll always be
Forever my love I give to thee

Our thoughts and hearts beat as one
It drives our spirit with amazing fun
So deep, so lasting our love doth talk
Sharing the journey in loves true walk

For every minute that comes our way
We bond even closer day by day
For even songs or words we hear
Sparks our love with feelings so near

This yearning we feel with loves true gift
Growth forever as we cuddle and kiss
This love we share enslaves our minds
Night and day our passion doth rhyme

Perfect and pure our hearts doth groan
Feeling such a love we've never known
For years loves fate hath passed us by
Now we smile with love inside

For deep within our love doth blend
This magic we share will never end
For our love will conquer all of time
Our love that was born is truly divine

Dexter L. Monroe

Loves Mighty Roar

You fill my days with laughter
You give your very best
To share our love together
One could feel so blessed

We hunger to hold and kiss
Our magic fills the air
A love that's very special
It's shared in loving care

Nothing in this world
Will ever change our minds
A love so deeply bonded
We'll hold forever in time

We know with out a doubt
Our love is true indeed
We answer every loving call
We hurry to every need

Love has truly entered
Our hearts forever more
We cling to every moment
Our loves a mighty roar

When the day is finally over
We snuggle in bed and share
Our bodies unite together
Blended with loving care

Dexter L. Monroe

Blissful Slumber

This magic we doth hold
Springs from our words so bold
From the waters of passionate hearts
We've felt this magic start

This blissful journey beyond
Will carry us beyond the dawn
For each day it's blooming more
A love we can truly adore

Slowly it's guiding our way
Giving without dismay
Pure and un-defiled
We'll rest in loves true trials

Tested through words of truth
Our hearts renew our youth
For fate has smiled again
Opening our hearts within

The un-known is beckoning now
With a loving covering shroud
Caressing our hearts it's applied
With gentle words we sigh

For maybe the sun did shine
The day our hearts did rhyme
For now we're burning with wonder
As we blissfully rest in slumber

Dexter L. Monroe

Treasure of Love

Treasures in life are rare
Some you could say are fare
With this treasure of love we found
Our hearts doth beat and pound

This beauty of love so deep
Our hearts will never weep
For nothing will come our way
To take this love away

This treasure of love so pure
Each breath doth draw us nearer
Hearts so filled with passion
Sealed in loves true fashion

For each day our love doth grow
Everlasting this love will flow
Like a river that winds so deep
This love forever we'll keep

Sown so deep within
Our minds doth truly spin
For our hearts doth truly know
The worth of this treasure we hold

So blessed our lives doth feel
For this love so deep and real
For silver and gold doth shine
But our treasure of love is divine

Dexter L. Monroe

Special Moments

Our silhouettes embrace the sky
As we snuggle O' so close
We pause to steal a kiss
A time we love to toast

A love so great and tender
Our hearts are joined as one
Forever and ever to be
With every setting sun

When evening dawns its face
We'll gently hold and stare
Embracing one another
We'll feel its loving care

Another day has ended
But our love shall never fade
The sun shall rise again
Our love was heaven made

Dexter L. Monroe

Loves True Realm

Forever night and day
My love will come your way
Sewn with care each hour
We'll share in loves true power

This beauty of love we found
We've entered loves true realm
So perfect in every way
In our hearts it will always stay

Our journey through life will come
Joined forever as one
For my wish will always be
To share my life with thee

Forever I'll try my best
My love will do the rest
For your heart shall always know
I love you from head to toe

Sincere in loves true fun
Our hearts will blend as one
Astounding in every way
Our passions will soar each day

For our hearts will truly say
Our love doth grow each day
So in love we'll always be
It was meant for you and me

Dexter L. Monroe

Sea Of Love

Dimly beyond the vale
Our lives like ships we'll sail
In romance our hearts will flee
Into a trance like loving sea

Our love shall ever abound
With spirits above the ground
Never in haste or waste
Will our love be found abased

Forever our hearts will sing
The songs of love shall ring
A rainbow of love we'll cast
Our hearts will dance so fast

We'll share this sea of love
A gift from heaven above
Our passions will rage within
Our stage of love begins

Unto a life so beautifully fare
Holding this love so rare
In love we'll soar beyond
Each day that breaks at dawn

Joined as one we'll sail
Our love shall never fail
This sea of love will be
Our anchor in time of need

Dexter L. Monroe

Dreaming With You

Beyond the magic of time
Love blooms within our minds
For each dream we share as one
Our love creates the fun

Rainbows fill the sky
On clouds of white we'll fly
Together in passionate bliss
Soaring with every kiss

The peaceful beat of our hearts
Shared with loves true darts
In fields of clover we'll lay
For our love doth guide the way

Our nakedness beams with a glow
Forever our love shall flow
Un-ending our wish will be
For each dream I'll share with thee

Dexter L. Monroe

Heaven Sent

Sounds of love, ring from above
We entreat each day, come what may
A love so deep, forever to stay

Hand in hand, we'll walk this land
Proudly we'll share a love so sweet
To love each other, a love complete

Ever giving our very best, never a test
Lives perfected with the beauty of love
Sent with truth, from heaven above

Day to day, we'll work and sow
Watching our love, watching it grow

Granting one wish, I'd give it to thee
A rainbow of flowers, nurtured with care
A love so deep, a love so rare

A day shall not pass, never to wonder
Never to doubt, you'll feel my love
Deeply endowed

I love thee

Dexter L. Monroe

Love Struck

On this quaint little bridge one day
We meant in grand array
Fate would have us collide
Hence meeting eye to eye

Seems as thought you choose
The very same path I strolled
For on that very day
We both had looked away

That second look we took
At swans swimming the brook
For that's all the time it would take
We bumped our heads in dismay

As I quickly found my feet
You sat upon your seat
"O' dear me!, I said
"Forgive me for bumping your head!

Then I reached out my hand
To help you gently stand
Something happened right then
A love began within

This magical spark we shared
In wonder we both did stare
For fate had come our way
A love did bloom that day

So each step you take through time
Love could come to dine
For fate could smile on you
The plan of love could bloom

Unusual this story may be
However it happened to me
The moral of this story should read
 "Love Struck" indeed

Dexter L. Monroe

Riches Of Love

By the tide's of night we'll dream
Together in love supreme
The darkness shall caress the ground
Our love forever will abound

We'll walk and share our hands
As the night inhale's the land
We'll frolic and share each kiss
Upon the star's we'll wish

For each day our love will grow
Never to fade or slow
With hearts that beat as one
We'll cherish our love and fun

The world will watch us soar
With a love we both adore
For with trust and truth we'll live
Honoring loves true gift

As the moon and sun trade places
Passionate times will embrace us
For our love will be the thunder
As we rise each day from slumber

For with hearts that beat the same
Our love forever will reign
For with powering forms we'll share
The riches of love and care

Dexter L. Monroe

The Wonder Of Love

Passionate thoughts, follow my days
Thinking of you and your loving ways

Your beauty glows, ever so bright
I embrace those thoughts, with loving delight

With every smile, you cast my way
It beams with love, day by day

Your words are magic, uttered so true
Spoken with love, for me and you

I cherish our times, with the deepest care
Your loving concerns, consume the air

This wondrous love, we embrace each day
It beams with passion, in every way

Your gentle touch, and sweet caress
I feel your love, I feel so blessed

You fill my days, and brighten my way
With every step, I take each day

You give me hope, with a love so dear
I cherish each moment, holding you near

Forever and ever, I will feel so blessed
Knowing our love, is truly the best

Dexter L. Monroe

One In Heart Forever

With every kiss we share
Our love doth fill the air
For with every hug we'll find
The longing for more each time

With loving hearts we'll climb
On clouds of love through time
For each day we'll soar much higher
We'll dine on loves desire

So deep, so strong within
Our love will always win
Together we'll share the power
For our love doth bloom like flowers

Our hearts shall be at peace
For our love will ever increase
We'll twine as one forever
Never shall our love be severed

Through work and loves true fun
We'll journey through life as one
Sharing in loves true play
Our passion will burn each day

With zest in loving desire
Nothing shall quench our fire
For our hearts can truly say
We're more in love each day

Dexter L. Monroe

Ever So True

When my eyes ascend on you
They linger with a love so true
For in every thought I yield
My love for you is sealed

Life would truly be amiss
If I'd never felt your kiss
For each kiss excites my soul
Your love doth make me whole

For each day we wake in bliss
At night we hold and kiss
So precious is every day
With your love I'll never stray

For our love was never planned
It happened so pure and grand
This happiness we both doth share
Came with love and care

For that day our hearts did sing
With hope and magic it brings
For love had truly rushed in
So complete we feel within

Every smile is set a glow
As we share this love we hold
For our love is ever so true
I'm so deeply in love with you!

Dexter L. Monroe

Love Finds A Way

There comes a time in life
When love replaces strife
For when our hearts are right
This love will be in sight

For this I can truly say
A love did come my way
A woman so special to me
I never thought I would see

But fate did smile one day
I'm happy in every way
For such a love as this
It's more than just a wish

For our hearts became as one
Never to be undone
This love we cherish and hold
Exceeds riches or gold

For how this came to be
It's forever a mystery to me
But this I truly know
Our love doth truly flow

Deeper and deeper we share
A love so pure and rare
For our hearts doth truly say
We're deeper in love each day

Dexter L. Monroe

Riches Or Gold

To gaze upon your countenance
Magically thrills my soul
Knowing each day our love will stay
A yearning to see it grow

Hour by hour we'll share our love
Bonded by word and deed
We'll strive in loving care
Fulfilling our deepest needs

One true wish we'll always be
Having your love each day
Side by side we'll sleep at night
We'll share our love this way

Your gentle kiss and sweet caress
I'll cherish forever and hold
A love so deep and bonded
Worth more then riches or gold

Our passions will always soar
With a love so great and true
I give to thee my very all
My loves for only you

Dexter L. Monroe

Echo's Of Love

So tranquil we find our peace
With hearts that share caprice
With love each moment released
Our passionate times increase

For our hearts doth speak aloud
With words forever endowed
So intense we fight to share
Our love so rich and rare

For our love does truly climb
Beyond space and time
Our hopes and dreams we share
With hearts of loving care

For times that we're apart
Our loves kept deep in heart
For every step we walk
Our hearts doth truly talk

The echo's of love we hear
Our hearts doth speak so clear
This bond of love we know
Forever our hearts will hold

Dexter L. Monroe

Sealed With A Kiss

O' thou fairest love of mine
Upon your love I dine
Your lips doth fly me away
To places unknown each day

Your touch holds loves true gift
Each day your love doth lift
It caresses my very soul
This love so deep I know

Your gleaming smile I cherish
Ones so cute and darish
For they shine with loving emotions
O' this loves devotion

The words you utter so sweet
Come from the heart so deep
Enticing with loves true wonder
For my heart will ever thunder

With passion your love doth show
Forever this love will grow
So immense, so deeply held
Forever I'm under your spell

Embracing each moment we share
For our hearts are blessed with care
This love so perfect and devout
Our hearts doth sing and shout

O' this great love we share
Nothing will ever compare
For this is our only wish
To hold and share each kiss

Dexter L. Monroe

Written In The Stars

Fate and time has placed us
Together in love this day
We finally found a love
forever shall it stay

We hold to every loving word
We utter and share so sweet
We're joined in perfect love
A love so dear to me

We laugh and share each day
Every hour is shared in bliss
We cling to every moment
Wanting to share a kiss

Your more than I could ask for
In every thing you do
All I ever dream about
Is spending each day with you

A love that was truly written
Deep within the stars
We hold to every moment
Never to fade apart

Every thing my heart will give
I'll share my all with you
You're my one and only dream
Forever a love so true

Dexter L. Monroe

Wavering Revelation

In youth our love did waiver
Seemingly from youth behavior
For true love was all but fleeting
Times at best entreating

Was this magic of love for dreaming?
Would we find true love so gleaming?
The clock of life spent on
Was true love forever gone?

This wonderment so bestowed
Ended with love that flowed
The beauty of love ascended
The days without love had ended

For this gift of loving fate
Was worth the days in wait
Forever this love shall reign
Setting our hearts to flame

For this love is worth more than gold
Forever to have and hold
O' this great love that's shared
Driven by loves true care

Forever so thankful are we
For this love that came to be
This love so deep within
Never shall we wonder again

Dexter L. Monroe

Loves True Power

O' those perfect nights
We share with loving might
This love so fashioned as one
Forever with loves true fun

For each hour we're truly alone
Our magical love is shown
For with loves endearing power
We'll soar together for hours

Sharing in every way
With minutes cherished in play
With love we'll truly find
A love beyond sublime

The passionate moments in bliss
We'll share with every kiss
For our hearts will pound with desire
Sharing our loves true fire

Our moans with groans of delight
Making love all through the night
The sun shall cast it's rays
In love we'll start each day

Forever we'll find new ways
To blend in loves true play
Our love will guide each hour
Forever with loves true power

Dexter L. Monroe

Armor of Love

My beautiful Princess, I surrender my all
I shall bow to thy wishes,never to fall.

With armor and shield, I will protect thy way
I will stand on guard, come what may.

I shall give to thee, my heart and my hand
We'll walk together, with loves great plan.

My arms will caress, like a cloak with care
Holding your love, a love so rare.

I shall fight this world, and keep it at bay
Nothing shall come, to harm thy way.

Our love will soar, above the clouds
Forever shall it be, forever and now.

A castle I will build, and give to thee
I will ask for your hand, upon my knees.

My Princess, my Queen, I grant this day
Forever shall I love thee, day by day.

Dexter L. Monroe

Eyes Of Loving Devotion

The twinkle and sparkle, cast in your eyes
Softly tells me of loves true cries
Those eyes of love and true emotion
Hold my heart in loving devotion

Lullabies that sing with every look
Flow like a mountain's meandering brook
Caressed with loves true trance
With hearts of love we'll dance

For they send such love filled signs
Reflecting your love that shines
That yearning to share as one
Never to be undone

Those love filled winks you cast
Forever in my heart they will last
Cherished as loves true gift
In loves true flight I'll drift

Forever to soar beyond
Your love so gently calms
That magic your eyes doth hold
Gleam with a love untold

O' that glorious day
Your eyes did speak and say
With one little wink I knew
Your love was forever true

Dexter L. Monroe

My Dearest Love

My love, my love, my dearest love
I love you more than the stars above
The moon, the sun, the planets on high
Nothing shall sway my loving tide

Your beauty doth shine in loves true way
O' this great love we share each day
Far or close we'll walk the path
Our love will guide and close the past

Forever our hearts will beat as one
Our lives will share in loves true fun
With every kiss of loves true fire
Our passions will raise higher and higher

For our touch will send loves true rage
Like magic our love will turn each page
This life we chose with pen in hand
Far exceeds loves true plan

So deep, so enchanting this love we share
Our love will grow with hearts of care
To this world we can say goodbye
Our love will soar beyond the sky

Arms embraced with love adorned
Our lives together we'll never morn
For our hearts will sing with angels above
My love, my love, my dearest love

Dexter L. Monroe

Peaceful Love

Finding you was such a dream
My life with you forever will beam
Never a day shall come to pass
For our love to stop and never last

Your love is so special, I hold it dear
Within my heart I feel you near
Day by day your always there
Giving your love in gentle care

Nothing shall ever stop our love
It grows each day like fitted gloves
O' how happy we both doth feel
Sharing a love so true and real

With every touch we gladly give
Happiness abounds with every kiss
The peaceful feeling to know such a love
Its truly blessed from heaven above

Time shall pass, but our love shall grow
Watered each day with a loving flow
Hearts so joined and bonded true
I give my all to only you

I come this day and want to say
Forever my love will always stay
Ever so thankful we're side by side
Our love forever will truly abide

Dexter L. Monroe

Never To Tarnish

A little bit higher, every day
Our love doth climb, in every way
Beyond the world our hearts doth soar
O' this great love, we truly adore

Thy countenance displayed in everyway
Your love forever I see each day
Your beauty doth lift my heart for thee
We found such a love, you and me

This yearning so deep to share it all
Your love for me shall never fall
Each moment we hold in loving care
Side by side, I want you there

Our journey through time, with love that rhymes
So deep our love forever will shine
No question shall ever enter in
Our love forever will truly win

Our hearts will thunder with every kiss
And our words of love we'll share in bliss
This enchanting love so dear and bold
Never shall it tarnish or turn to old

This love so magical we share so deep
We rest our hearts in loves true beats
Together our hearts and minds will be
Forever as one, just you and me

Dexter L. Monroe

Candle Light Nights

By candle light, we'll spend the night
Powering our love in shear delight
Our passions will soar, like never before
Locked in love, we'll hear it roar

Our minds will lock in worlds unknown
Our bodies will shutter with every moan
Moment by moment embraced with care
We'll find a rhythm and gently share

As the candle flickers and burns down low
Our love begins to really show
Faster our hearts will pump and plea
With every breathe, a love so deep

With all our might, we'll hold so tight
Forever in memory a love so right
With every kiss, our tongues will mingle
Exploring in love with every tingle

Over and over we'll give and play
Our love will turn from night to day
O' how sweet the nights will be
Forever and ever to be with thee

Loving all night the time doth fly
The sun did rise, to our great surprise
We loved all night, sharing each kiss
Again O' please, will be our wish

Dexter L. Monroe

Forever To Hold

To live each day at your side
Comes with such a loving pride
So thankful I shall ever be
For all the love you granted me

On the wings of a white dove
We found such a love
Hearts so bonded and deeply sown
Deep felt words we can only moan

O' how I love thee, my dearest one
Life with you is so much fun
The times with you in loving play
We'll live and love each glorious day

How enchanting our nights will be
Giving my love to only thee
We'll sing each day a lullaby
A love so sweet, never to die

Our love forever will share this theme
You're the one that walks my dreams
Night and day when our thoughts do teary
Knowing such a love will make us merry

Blessed with a love so dear and grand
We'll walk each day with loves great plan
Forever to share when growing old
My heart is yours, forever to hold

Dexter L. Monroe

Moon Light Magic

Under the moon and stars so bright
We'll kiss and hold each other so tight
Our passion will build with a mighty roar
Into the stars our love will soar

Every touch that's shared during night
Will send our hearts in total flight
A wanting for more to ever last
Higher then the stars we'll gently pass

Our journey through time will be divine
A love so great, forever we'll dine
Kisses so sweet will taste like wine
Holding forever, no need for time

How sensual our love will always be
Loving beneath the stars we'll see
Our bodies we'll share with nothing a dare
Sharing each moment with loving care

Our eyes will twinkle with stars on high
Lifting our hearts above the sky
With each consuming thrust we make
Our bodies will shutter in awesome quake

O' the nights we share this way
Forever our love will always stay
Raging within our hearts and minds
With the moon above our love will shine

Dexter L. Monroe

Titanic Love

O' to cast my eyes upon your beauty
Your burning passion I perceive, the lingering touch
That fire that consumes our every want
A love never before captured deep within
The fervor, the need to win.

Let us share in ecstasies we fondly desire
Delighting in perfect bliss with every kiss
Your sweet nectar, I find desirably consuming
Your heavenly body storms within my mind
I lay my head upon your breast's, I rest.

Titanic is our love, higher than the tops of mountains
We soar to heights never before touched-- we pause
Not in any measure will the mind conceive
Intensely we share, a love that breathes

Your beauty unfolds like a flower budding in delight
I shall cherish our days with stars on high
Higher than the eagles spread forth to fly
We love, we kiss, we play-- magic dawns each day
Forever will our love abound, with every song and sound

Our hearts will twine as one, boldly our love will shine
Dwelling forever in time, our love will always rhyme
Never to cease, ever giving, our love we'll share forever

Dexter L. Monroe

Soaring Passion

My dearest loving Princess
For in you my love doth dwell
My eternal and faithful heart
Rings with loves true bells

I the steeple, solid and strong
I prey thee to hide within and belong
I shall be your Knight of loving armor
Spinning our love with a golden arbor

This shining love I give to thee
I bid thee this loving plea
Let us soar beyond enchanting stars
To our castle of dreams set afar

Beyond the moons we shall collide
This shall be our by and by
With lullabies and fields coated with color
We'll trade our love one to another

Quenching never our soaring desires
Higher and higher in loves true fire
Spiraling beyond space and void
Hurling our love, bonded in joy

Our forms unite in loving rain
For this shall be our loving game
To hold forever through eons of time
Together forever our love shall rhyme

Dexter L. Monroe

Upon One Knee

So entranced is my every thought
Of this love we share and sought
Through the wiles of life we endured
To keep our love secure

This love that's with stood life's storms
Through time and days it was born
So enchantingly filling our desires
As one we share the same fire

Hearts bonded in words of truth
O' such a love we induce
This love of pure light within
Shall never fade or dim

Savoring every caress
Knowing our love is so blessed
Our passion glows in each utter
With words we consume like butter

Sharing feelings we both doth melt
For our love is so deep and indwelt
In each sigh our feelings are shared
For in nothing else we care

Only to be as one
Forever as mates un-done
For now I can truly ask
Will you marry me at last?

Dexter L. Monroe

71

Autumn Leaves

The leaves of autumn doth change
With colors of fire they flame
For the time shall truly come
In love we'll mate as one

The journey through time we shared
Our love grew sweeter with care
Each day it grew even more
For in love our hearts doth roar

When I think of what we share
Forever at your side with care
Our passions we'll be unleashed
Our love will be released

For one in heart and mind
Together forever through time
In love and fun and tears
Our love will guide for years

So enchanting in every way
Growing deeper in love each day
O' this wonderful love we found
For our magic of love abounds

Sweeter with every hour
We share in loves true power
So deep, so perfect and pure
Forever our love will endure

Dexter L. Monroe

Loves True Psalms

Love hath awakened my soul
Ever burning out of control
Born with loves true light
Lifting our hearts in delight

O' this great love that bonds
Flow's eternal with loves true psalms
So exciting it makes each day
Our love that's shared and craved

Thou hast made me whole I can say
For all the love you display
Nothing in this world I want most
Only to hold you close

Your beauty un-matched I see
It means the world to me
For thou hast given your all
Knowing this I stand so tall

Whispering gently to your ear
I love you so much my dear
Never shall I turn aside
In your love I shall always confide

Dexter L. Monroe

Our Secret Hiding Place

A gentle breeze surrounds us
As we walk a forest one day
Deep within we'll walk
Loving along the way

We'll journey to find a lake
And ponder the beauty of blue
Then we'll find a special spot
One for loving you

We'll sit upon a fallen tree
Caressing all the while
Our minds will lock with passion
Sharing a loving smile

Nature will only clothe us
Doing as we may
Free among the trees
We'll sing and love and play

This will be our wish
Our secret hiding place
Deep within the forest
we'll love the day away

Dexter L. Monroe

The Sound Of Love

Our love resembles the sound
Of flutes and harps in play
O' that glorious day
For this love that came our way

How deep our love is shared
Our hearts are bonded with care
We share our hearts each day
Searching in everyway

To give our utmost all
We entreat each loving call
With enticing words of dare
Passionate times we share

This enchanting life together
We'll enjoy our days forever
Forever my love will be
Given to only thee

Our days will gently pass
For our love will surely last
With thankful hearts and minds
We'll share this love divine

For truly our hearts do beat
Feeling a love so sweet
Forever and ever I'll say
I Love You more each day

Dexter L. Monroe

The Lasting Embrace

O' that day of our embrace
For truly our hearts did race
Fulfilling every desire
Our hearts did rage with fire

For every dream came true
To be holding only you
Caressing for hours that day
We loved the night away

With blazing passion we found
Our love so truly sound
Forever our hearts would say
I will share my love each day

We'll cherish the minutes that come
Trading our love in fun
To give our loving best
Sharing a life so blessed

Memories we'll share so sweet
Embracing each night we sleep
Waking each day to find
A love so truly divine

For every day we'll know
And feel a love that grows
For a love so real and true
I give my heart to you

Dexter L. Monroe

Letter Of Love

With pen in hand I write
This letter of love tonight
For its addressed to the one I love
Carried on the wings of a dove

O' Dearest sweet love of mine
Upon your love I dine
Your beauty and love so fare
No other shall ever compare

Each smile you cast my way
Fills my soul each glorious day
With deep emotions I feel
Your love so true and real

How I yearn to feel your touch
The touch I love so much
Your warm and gentle caress
Forever I'll feel so blessed

For the love you share with me
It grants my every need
Every kiss that you impart
Forever will touch my heart

For each day that's spent with you
My feelings are never blue
And with these words I say
I love you more each day

My world is so complete
Knowing a love so sweet
Forever I hope you'll see
You mean the world to me

Dexter L. Monroe

Our Dreams

Let us dream our dreams together
Forever sharing this gift
Hand in hand in a colorful land
Our bodies will hold and kiss

Through time and space of mind
We'll journey upon our way
Beauty we'll find, we'll drink the wine
Sharing our dreams each day

A world of color and magic we'll share
Drifting through places unknown
We'll dance and sing along the way
Caressing in love we'll roam

With flight, we'll soar through time
To places so grand and dear
Valleys and mountains we'll share on high
Sharing our dreams so clear

Forever we'll spend our lives in bliss
As we hold this wondrous gift
We'll pause and bond in every way
Never a day we'll miss

With this thought, we'll make one wish
To dream our dreams of fun
Holding and sharing our dreams together
Forever to be as one

Dexter L. Monroe

Apple Of My Eye

These words of love I give to you
For you're the one I love so true
You make my days so sunny and bright
Sharing your love with all your might

The time we share is wonderfully sweet
My life with you is so complete
For every day your loves displayed
I tingle inside with loves array

Your more than the apple of my eye
You're the reason for living, never to die
To feel your love in such a great way
Forever to hold and cherish each day

For every smile you thrust my way
It's a smile of love forever to stay
Your heart doth speak through words you share
Ever so gently with loving care

Happiness fills my heart and soul
To know such a love to have and hold
For ever and ever I want you close
Side by side, like loves true ghost

Forever and ever I give to thee
A love beyond the eye can see
And with these final words conveyed
I love you more then words can say

Dexter L. Monroe

Loves Great Shroud

Our life of love so boldly says
We'll hold this love through times of stress
We'll walk through valleys hand in hand
Knowing this love was Gods true plan

For each day we feel the mystery unfold
Of such a love to share and hold
Deep within our hearts speak loud
O' such a love like an enduring shroud

It covers our thoughts night and day
O' this great love will guide our way
Like ships at sea with lights at night
We'll share this love with hearts so bright

Steady is our path of a love so dear
For with every touch our love shines clear
Truly forever as one in heart
Sharing each day the love we impart

For you love me, and I loveth you
With loves true colors so pure and true
For all of this makes my world complete
O' such a love so beautifully sweet

Nothing shall ever hinder my mind
For my love is all yours till the end of time
For each day I'll cherish at your beckoned side
Forever in this love we'll both reside

Dexter L. Monroe

The Wishing Well

From the wishing well of life
We raised a bucketfull
Full of wondrous waters
A love we both doth know

We drink upon that love
Sharing a cup a day
A drink that's pure in love
Forever shall it stay

Truly we feel it's magic
In everything we do
We cling to every moment
That's shared by me and you

Drink my dearest love
We'll share a cup or two
Taste upon my love
Given to only you

A love we'll draw together
Sealed from heaven above
The wishing well of life
Forever to be in love

Dexter L. Monroe

Sublime Love

A song in our hearts did sing
We heard the bells that ring
For love was in the air
We found a love so rare

We melted together as one
With passionate times of fun
Enchanting with every kiss
We entered a life of bliss

This love we'd found so great
Forever to be as mates
Never again to wander
Never again to ponder

Our lives became as one
Like rays from the golden sun
Perfect in every way
To love and to hold each day

For life with you by far
Compares to the light of a star
Forever your love doth shine
It's truly a love sublime

Dexter L. Monroe

Eternal Pictures of Love

Time with you is utterly dear
O' such a love that draws me nearer
For each loving smile we share
Our minds doth keep it there

For when we close our eyes
Those smiles of love abide
Picture's within our minds
A love that's yours and mine

Perfect in every way
We think a like each day
One in heart and mind
Our love doth truly rhyme

O' what a love we have
Bonded in hearts so glad
To share such a love sublime
In love we'll swim through time

For our love will soar up yonder
Growing each day even fonder
Yielding our hearts in one desire
Kindling forever our loving fire

For one in heart we'll grow
Eternally our love will show
To share such a love with you
There's nothing I'd rather do

Dexter L. Monroe

Wish Upon A Star

Stars that twinkle in the heavens on high
We'll share their light with a gentle sigh
Forever glowing and sent our way
A light so pure, forever to stay

When the skies are dark the magic begins
We'll lay together the best of friends
Our eyes will twinkle with the stars above
Gazing at the heavens, we'll share our love

For a wish we'll make as a star doth fall
Our eyes will follow, watching it all
Grant us our wish O' shooting star
A wish, a wish, it comes from afar

Our days will be merry, loving and dear
Holding the moments year after year
Our hearts, our souls, our minds as one
Enjoying the stars we'll find our fun

Day by day our wish will guide
Forever we'll hold our wish and sigh
O' star of night, share your light
Grant us eternal love this night

Dexter L. Monroe

Love Preserved

A fountain of love that dwells within
We smile each day to let it win
Perfected in love our hearts doth say
Our love will keep the world at bay

Times with troubles I'm sure we'll greet
We'll use our love in great defeat
Hearts united and joined as one
We'll fight to keep our love and fun

With trusting hearts we'll give each day
Forever and ever to guide our way
Safe and sure our lives will be
Hand in hand we'll walk so free

Gold and silver is linked to greed
Our love will shine without that need
For every step we're bound as one
Never a life to be un-done

We'll journey each day in loves display
Happy and merry along the way
With a love so honest, pure and true
All my love is given to you

Day and night forever to hold
Our love we'll rage ever so bold
We'll seek in truth loves great plan
Sharing our hearts, hand in hand

Dexter L. Monroe

A Thousand Candles

O' thou dearest lover
Hear thy heart thunder with wonder
Awaken thy soul from slumber
For flowers doth bloom
And my love doth swoon

For my eyes doth see your fire
That burning so deep desire
A love that fills each day
This love you send my way

O' that sense of loves true plan
Enchanting forever this love so grand
Our flames doth flicker with every word
For a thousand candles burn like wood
In times of storm our love withstood

Our hearts and minds doth truly chassin
This love we share in true relation
For it beams above the stars on high
Our love doth grow beyond the sky

So intense our dreams doth show the way
Hand and hand we walk and play
Together we share this love so bold
Dream my dear with loves true hold

For each day we smile in loving array
With words of love that flow each day
For upon this love our hearts doth ride
Forever this love will truly abide

Dexter L. Monroe

Romantic Fun

Forever we'll walk and play
Through gardens of love each day
With flowers that bloom so fare
The scent of love we'll share

In hobbies we'll join as one
To share our love in fun
In laughter our hearts will say
I love you more each day

For quiet times will come
Romantically under the sun
Those special times we'll share
Nothing will ever compare

For to spend each day with you
There's nothing I'd rather do
For all the times we'll share
Giving our love with care

To help and guide our way
We'll give with love each day
In happiness our love will show
Forever our love will grow

In love and fun and play
We'll give our all each day
For our hearts will gladly flow
With a love we'll always know

Dexter L. Monroe

Forever, Forever, Forever

Forever to be my hope and dreams
Forever to love will be our theme
Forever to share in loving need
Forever to give in loving deed
Forever we'll share and grant with care
Forever to be a lasting pair
Forever joined in total bliss
Forever to kiss will be our wish
Forever to hold your hand each day
Forever and ever at my side to stay
Forever to love and show our faith
Forever to give with Gods true grace
Forever to make our lives complete
Forever a love so truly sweet
Forever to feel and make it known
Forever to never feel alone
Forever and ever in consuming love
Forever our hearts will sing like doves
Forever with love I give to thee
Forever to you my love is free
Forever our hearts will yearn each day
Forever to give come what may
Forever to caress with a love so true
Forever our hearts to be renewed
Forever to feel your gentle touch
Forever delighted to give as much
Forever to see your loving smile
Forever to lay and kiss awhile
Forever our hearts will gladly say
"Forever, Forever, Forever"

Dexter L. Monroe

Above The Clouds

Days shall pass with a love that last
Our love forever will grow
Clouds on high, we'll touch the sky
Embracing moments our hearts doth fly

Higher and higher our love will ascend
Reaching the heavens above
Inhaling each kiss we'll never miss
On the wings of a dove we'll fly

The fire we'll feel with great appeal
With a love that burns inside
I'll live each day, giving your way
Just to see you smile

Let me hold this thought so dear
To love you more each day
We'll sing and dance, share in romance
Our love will always stay

Now and forever you'll share my wish
Granting your love each day
With hugs and kisses we'll touch and know
Our love, will gently flow

I give to thee with every breath
A love forever to be
Come with me and share this love
Blessed by the heavens above

Dexter L. Monroe

Beholding You

When my eyes ascend on you
They linger with a love so true
For every thought I yield
My love for you is sealed

Life would truly be amiss
If I'd never felt your kiss
For each kiss excites my soul
Your love doth make me whole

For each morn we'll wake in bliss
At night we'll hold and kiss
So precious is every day
With your love I'll never stray

For our love was never planned
It happened so pure and grand
The serenity we both now share
Came with love and care

For that day our hearts did sing
With hope and magic it brings
For love had truly rushed in
So complete we feel within

Every smile is set a glow
As we share this love we hold
For our love is ever true
I'm so deeply in love with you

Dexter L. Monroe

Eternal Love

Enchanting and ecstatic I give to thee
My endearing love gladly with glee
Our moments entwined with a love divine
Better than the taste of ageless wine,
We dine

Our hearts do rage in passion un-caged
Twined together in loves true maze
We walk this path, hand in hand
Our love doth swim through space and land

Hour upon hour we'll feed our lives
With a love that's sent by Gods blue sky
Forever our hearts will climb the soar
We'll reach new heights like never felt before

Sharing a love through years and time
Blessed with a love that truly rhymes
Everlasting we'll give our all
Bonded in heart we'll stand so tall

O' this love that we doth know
It burns forever with such a glow
Our cares will be that every desire
Is fulfilled in love, never to tire

I give to thee with every breath
Forever to share and do my best
To impart my love so deep and true
To love each day that's spent with you

Dexter L. Monroe

Loves True Light

For our hearts doth truly spin
With our love so deep within
For nothing shall stand in our way
We'll live as one each day

For we'll live in loves true plan
Forever our love will stand
A fortress of love we'll share
Guarded with love's true care

For my Princess you'll always be
All my love I give to thee
Forever I'll be your Knight
Shining in loves true light

Forever our hearts will beat
As one with love so deep
For each day we'll find the chance
To share in loves romance

Each moment so special in time
Our love will soar and climb
Beyond this world we know
With the winds of love we'll flow

Soaring with every stroke
In loves true flight we'll float
We'll journey for hours together
In loves true light forever

Dexter L. Monroe

Beyond The End Of Time

For ever and ever and ever
Our love we'll share together
For the words "For Ever" mean
Eternally no ending shall be

For this love we share so deep
Together in loves true sleep
Our hearts forever entwined
Beyond the end of time

Never my dear, let your heart worry
Confide in our love with steady courage
For this I can truly say
Trust in our love each day

When ever your feeling low
Cling to my love and hold
For within your heart I live
Forever my love I'll give

There's nothing in this world I desire
Only your love to share our fire
Nothing shall quench the flames
Of this love we share the same

For each day we journey through life
Never worry or think in strife
For our love will keep us strong
For one in heart we belong

Dexter L. Monroe

Beyond The Stars

For each day that's spent with you
My heart is truly renewed
Renewed by you with love
With angels that sing above

For never a day shall pass
That our love won't make it last
For time did stop one day
Our love now guides the way

Mountains and hills we'll climb
With love we'll swim through time
We'll frolic through places unknown
Sharing our love with moans

Our passion will truly climb
Within our hearts and minds
Each kiss will set the stage
Together with loves true rage

In loves true power we'll share
What ever our bodies can bare
We'll escape this world we know
To places of love we'll go

Our minds will take us there
To worlds beyond compare
For upon this love we'll dine
Beyond the stars that shine

Dexter L. Monroe

Sealed Hearts

This love I cherish with you
Has made my life so new
For it's touched my very soul
For it's you that's made me whole

That longing to share such a love
Was sent from heaven above
You impart such a trueness of heart
I was clothed by your love from the start

Our love has gathered strength
For daily this love we drink
We're feed like babes in arms
We'll keep our love from harm

The doors of this world we'll shut
We'll boast of our love and strut
We'll keep our love secure
Our love should know no fear

In each word we'll share our hearts
Trading in loves true darts
This beauty of love we share
We'll hold forever with care

For nothing shall change my heart
Even in times apart
We've won the ultimate test
With love that beats the rest

Forever we've sealed our hearts
That day our love did start
For truly I'm happy to know
Our love forever will grow

Dexter L. Monroe

Sea of Loving Desire

Our eyes doth speak with wonder
Twinkling with hearts that thunder
Our love doth burn with fire
For it's our sea of loving desire

Relentless is this love we know
Carried with the winds that blow
For our hearts doth chant in song
This love we found so strong

Moments of time will linger
With fates true loving finger
How consuming this love we share
Each kiss is planted with care

This passionate rage we entreat
Sparks our hearts to beat
Pumping true love each day
Never shall it flee away

For each loving caress we impart
A yearning for more doth start
This love of ours doth bind
It rhymes in our hearts sublime

For each hour I share with thee
Our love forever will be
Enduring so deep and sound
Forever our love will abound

Dexter L. Monroe

Blooming Flowers

If I could be a flower
My love would bloom each hour
For if you were a flower by me
My love you'd always see

For with every wind that blew
Our stems would snuggle true
Forever we'd twine and share
We'd bloom with love and care

Colorful our blooms would be
For the world would truly see
Our love planted so deep
We'd share in loves true sleep

For every morning we'd feel
The dew of love so real
Growing and twining as one
Blooming with loving fun

For each day the sun doth shine
We'd bloom with love divine
For the rain would feed our hearts
Never our stems would part

Our routs would mingle below
Forever we'd never let go
Blooming with you each day
Our love forever would stay

Dexter L. Monroe

By the Sea of Love

By the sea of love we'll go
Sharing this love we know
We'll journey loves truth path
Our love eternal will last

With hearts so truly a lined
We'll kiss and taste the wine
The wine of loves true fate
Forever to be as mate's

With our hearts of love galore
Forever we'll feel the roar
With songs of love each day
Our hearts we'll gently say

O' how I love you dear
Your love doth draw me nearer
For together in hearts we'll walk
With words of love we'll talk

We'll share our hearts of joy
With words of love we employ
We'll seek and find new ways
To share our love each day

With hours of passion we'll find
Our bodies we'll mingle and dine
For happy our lives we'll stay
By the sea of love each day

Dexter L. Monroe

Sunset Love

Along the river, we'll walk the trails
Watching the sun go down
This is our time to share our love
Making our world go round

We'll find a bench to sit and glare
Avoiding this world with all its cares
We'll hold and kiss, touch and share
Watching the sun go down

The sun will dip to waters edge
Closer we'll draw in loving pledge
Feeling our love so rare and true
Watching the sun go down

You'll stand and giggle and find my lap
You'll sit with a hint of dare
O' those moments with out a care
Watching the sun go down

Our love will peak as we doth speak
Holding so close and growing weak
Forever and ever a love so sweet
Watching the sun go down

The warmth of day will pass away
The sun shall slip and fall
We'll linger there in loving care
Watching the sun go down

Dexter L. Monroe

The Winds Of Love

O' this endless love we know
Through loves true winds it blows
With raging hearts we feel
Our passionate times revealed

Like trees we bend and sway
Romancing with love each day
This magical gift we know
So deeply in love we grow

My eyes behold and see
How great a love should be
To never doubt within
Our love shall always win

O' those great winds that blew
Forever a love so true
Our hearts are calmed each day
Knowing this love will stay

For now in my heart I feel
This love so tender and real
With fire our hearts doth kindle
Our love shall never dwindle

For this love we both doth know
Forever to share and hold
O' those great winds that blew
This love to me and you

Dexter L. Monroe

Carved In Stone

Once in a life time span
We cling to loves true plan
For this I can truly say
I love you more each day

This love we found so sweet
It drives our hearts to beat
So perfect and gently endowed
Our love doth cry aloud

For each hour could pass away
In silence we could sit and play
For without one word we'd know
This love forever we'll hold

This magic of love's true bliss
So consuming is every kiss
For the letter "L" in love
Was sent from heaven above

How sensual a love we found
Forever our hearts will pound
With love's true magic in time
Our love will truly shine

For each word that we doth moan
Its' carved in love's true stone
Placed with loves true care
Within our hearts to share

Dexter L. Monroe

Castle Of Dreams

My princess so loving fare
O' this devouring love we share
With loves burning desire
Our hearts are set a fire

This yearning so deep inside
On this love we'll ever ride
Beyond the moon above
To the gates of heavens love

This love so bold and sweet
Forever our hearts will beat
Bonded forever as one
Never to be un-done

Come hither my fairest my love
To this castle of dreams above
Our love will carry us on high
Beyond the deep blue sky

O' this love so grand
Fulfills our loving demand
With every gentle kiss
We make another wish

Together we pray and ask
This love forever will ever last
Beyond the hours of time
On this love forever we'll dine

Dexter L. Monroe

With Loving Thunder

O' how our love doth thunder
With words of beauty and wonder
Shared forever in number
We embrace each night in slumber

Your magical touch of love
Is given with every hug
Ascending from heaven above
Our love forever so snug

Our hearts are joined in every thought
Our passionate times so very hot
For every loving kiss is sought
Nothing shall come to not

O' what a love so beautiful and true
Giving my heart to only you
Never a day of feeling blue
Only your love will ever do

How great the feeling, your love doth call
Imparted each day, never to fall
A feeling so good and nothing small
I stand with you so proud and tall

Your love is shared, beyond compare
A heart felt love that's given with care
Forever and ever we shall share
A love so perfect, a love so rare

Dexter L. Monroe

Thirsting For Thee

I thirst each day to be with you
To taste your love so rare and true
For each word of passion we share
Never shall we know despair

With a spirit of loving devotion
We share in loves true motion
Carried beyond the stars
So perfect is this love of ours

That yearning we hold so deep
Is our love forever to keep
Those flames of passion we bare
Forever will burn with care

The sparkle in life each day
Will come from words we say
For upon this love we'll dwell
Forever to keep it well

For each hour that slips away
We're deeper in love each day
This beautiful love that abides
As one in heart we confide

For nothing shall sway our minds
For each beat of hearts doth rhyme
Sealed with the flames of desire
We share with loves true fire

Dexter L. Monroe

The Gift of Love

To feel such love within
Our hearts forever swim
This sea of love is ours
Sealed within the stars

Our hearts will ever sing
To this love so fare we cling
For this will be our wish
To live and love in bliss

To share our love each day
This gift of love will stay
Buried within our hearts
This love shall never depart

For we shall always know
This gentle loving flow
With a love so truly blessed
Our hearts will share and rest

With faithful loving care
We hold this love so rare
Bonded in every way
A life without dismay

How wonderful life can be
To share my love with thee
Forever our hearts will feel
This love so true and real

For the years will come and go
My love will always show
With spoken words I'll say
I love you more each day

Dexter L. Monroe

Roaring Passion

Each gentle touch will sing a song
A song of love as the night grows long
Our hearts will blend to be as one
Hugging and giving in all our fun

Minute by minute the fire we'll feel
Burning so deep in loving appeal
Our hearts will pound at a loving pace
To finally beat like running a race

With every kiss and move we make
We'll find new ways to give and take
Holding in rhythm our pace will grow
Faster and faster our love will show

O' the feelings that we entreat
O' this magic of a love so deep
The moans the moves will tell us so
Gently we'll share in letting go

Sigh's will join in this time so sweet
Rocking together in loving heat
Gently we'll share in loving caress
We'll fade together in loving rest

Dexter L. Monroe

Sufficient and Forever

Nothing shall stand in our way
Our love shall guide each day
Sufficient and forever more
O' this great love we adore

This revelation that came to pass
Knowing that our love shall last
Beyond the stars of time
Our love forever will shine

For with hearts of love the same
Our world together will flame
For kindling we'll share and add
Our words of love so glad

For each day we'll find new ways
Setting our passions a blaze
The magic of every touch
Sharing and giving so much

Deeper in love with each step
Never ever to forget
How great a love we found
Resounding in our hearts that pound

For we'll lift each others hearts
With love each day we'll impart
For with hearts and minds unchanged
Forever our love will reign

Dexter L. Monroe

Resting In Bliss

O' the sweetness of your gentle kiss
Your words of passion speak with bliss
Ever so happy you make my life
Never to spend our time in strife

The wonderful love that we doth share
Emanates so deep with hearts of care
For everyday that's shared with you
Forever our love will be like new

With this promise, I give to thee
All of my love for you to see
Now and forever, this is my wish
Our love shall grow with every kiss

We join our hearts with every deed
To answer each call of loving need
A love so cherished and blessed each day
From heaven above, this I pray

The words we share each night and day
Are laced with love in all we say
When the sun falls deep and night begins
Our passions will soar deep within

Sharing this time in loving embrace
Our bodies will join at a loving pace
Our sleep will come with peaceful rest
Knowing each day we gave our best,
Caressing now we rest

Dexter L. Monroe

The Best Love

For this is my only plea
That forever your loves with me
To guide me through each day
Sharing your loving ways

For my heart is truly yours
Forever my love will endure
To make you happy each day
Secure in every way

My heart will truly be glad
Never to see you sad
For this I can truly say
You'll have my love each day

For years will come and go
But my love for you will grow
For this you'll truly see
My loves only given to thee

For every day we share
Our love will rage with care
The fires of passion will burn
With love our world will turn

With words of " I Love You"
Forever you'll know it's true
Each day we'll love and caress
Knowing our loves the best

Dexter L. Monroe

Moon Love Reflection

There's a face upon the moon
They say it's a man and assume
For this is truly wrong
It's love that shines so strong

For the face we see at night
Mirrors our love in flight
Carried through space and time
It's our love that truly shines

No matter where we are
It shines like a beacon afar
Reflecting the love we share
We ponder and look and stare

For this mystery of love in the sky
In loving gentleness we sigh
Thinking of the love we impart
This love we carry in our hearts

For each time we see that face
It can start our hearts to race
To know such a love we share
Reflected by the moon with care

Dexter L. Monroe

Harbor Of Fate

Upon the shores of eternal
I shall write in my heart a journal
For all of my love is yours
For you I truly adore

The serenity of knowing your love
It's the best there ever was
For there's nothing I want most
Then this love we share and toast

Moon light nights we'll share
As one beyond compare
Our love shall team with pride
Upon our life long ride

Together in love secure
Our love will help us endure
For riches shall never claim
This love we hold the same

Magical and truly unique
Bonded forever so deep
Blessed by the hand of fate
Our love was not a mistake

Our destiny was sure and strong
Our love is where it belongs
It's scribed within our hearts
Never shall it ever depart

Dexter L. Monroe

Loves True Rhyme

O' such a passionate love
Granted to us from above
Our hearts thus beat the same
As one in loves true rain

The magic of every embrace
Sets our hearts to race
That roar of thundering passion
Shall never grow old fashion

This magical mystery of love
Is carried on the wings of a dove
For within our hearts as one
Our love goes beyond the sun

For each kiss our lips doth trade
We seal our love each day
This wondrous love we found
Nothing could be more sound

For contentment fills our day's
Our love is molded like clay
Fired with word's of love
Forever to hold as enough

With enduring sighs we'll plead
Our love shall guide and lead
For each moment we share in time
Our love forever shall rhyme

Dexter L. Monroe

Tranquil Hearts

Soaring to heavens height
Our love is like flying a kite
Beyond the sky's of blue
I'm so in love with you

Through clouds of cottony haze
Our love is majestically raised
For each day it's lifted higher
Carried by the winds of desire

With peaceful and tranquil hearts
We'll share in Cupids darts
Hearts so perfectly entwined
Soaring together through time

No strings will guide our way
Our love will never fray
For the magical winds of love
Soar higher then the wings of a dove

Floating with a love so free
It was meant for you and me
Rising beyond heavens gates
Our love was sealed by fate

Blissful is our eternal ride
On the winds of loves true tide
Together through all of time
We'll soar with a love divine

Dexter L. Monroe

www.ingramcontent.com/pod-product-compliance
Lightning Source LLC
Chambersburg PA
CBHW051813040426
42446CB00007B/654